T0208367

SPIRITUAL
MECHANICS

SPIRITUAL
MECHANICS

TANZIA MUSTAFA, MD

ARCHWAY
PUBLISHING

Archway Publishing books may be ordered through booksellers or by contacting:

Archway Publishing
1663 Liberty Drive
Bloomington, IN 47403
www.archwaypublishing.com
1 (888) 242-5904

ISBN: 978-1-4808-3963-2 (sc)
ISBN: 978-1-4808-3962-5 (hc)
ISBN: 978-1-4808-3964-9 (e)

Library of Congress Control Number: 2016919550

Print information available on the last page.

Archway Publishing rev. date: 11/23/2016

This book is dedicated to the memory of my mother, the late Mrs. Nazma Mustafa.

CONTENTS

CONTENTS

INTRODUCTION

My journey began at the capital city of a developing country. My childhood was blessed with an amazing mother, who was an undaunted spirit. She had answers to all my existential questions: Who am I? What is this world? Why are we here? Her answers were straightforward: You are a servant of God's purpose. This world is a testing ground for how you serve God's purpose. We are here to better ourselves so that we come closer to God.

I remember my mother's frantic efforts to keep my hair free from head lice, which is still an epidemic in school going children of developing countries. The only way she could lure me into sitting still so that she could comb my hair and search for those tiny insects and their eggs was to tell me stories. By the time I was a third grader, I knew all the biblical stories of Adam and Eve, Noah and his boat, Abraham and Ishmael, Joseph and his brothers, and Mary and Christ, as well as Buddha, Ramakrishnan, and so on and so forth. No wonder it was a never-ending process for my mother, as my hair was never free of those insects. There were no lice-killing shampoos back in the seventies. My mother's storytelling continued till I was a teenager.

By the time I was a young adult, I became confused with my religious beliefs, superimposed with my newfound knowledge of theories of evolution, Marxism, and modern science. I grappled to reconcile all this information and make sense of this world. Far from being easy, it became more and more difficult a process. The more I educated myself, the more confused I became. I remained fragmented for a long time. By saying fragmented I mean my way of living my life was different than the way I perceived my life should be lived. I continued to live my life according to my religious upbringing, although I did not see the scientific basis of the existence of God—the hard-core statistically analyzed evidence that is. Some rituals in my religion I continued to practice, although I did not find them scientific. Some rituals involved slaughtering of animals, which I found revolting. However, I did not want to discard my belief system, as I hoped I would find those answers one day.

Much later, I became a medical doctor and decided to specialize in mental science and its diseases. I believe my original existential quest for the truth and meaning of life has contributed to my finally becoming a psychiatrist. I treated thousands of my patients and their mental anguishes, prescribed medications, and counseled them for their emotional turmoil. I familiarized myself with modern concepts of the mind, its malfunctions, and how to diagnose and treat them. I was aware even from my medical school days that the key to understanding this universe may lie in understanding our own mental processes.

So you might think that I have the answer to that ever-burning question of existence in this planet, but I don't—not even close. Even with all the twenty-first-century modern technologies, we are able to see the brain but still unable to locate the mind. We are able to locate numerous different parts of the brain responsible for certain functions of the mind; however, we are not able to find the part that assimilates all the information and gives rise to the constant thinking process and emotional waves we experience in both our waking hours and when we're asleep.

If I have to use a metaphor, I would use a computer. Suppose that I am working on a computer. It is programmed to take a picture of me, and it recognizes me. I look at this computer with my eyes, and the picture of the computer is transmitted to the visual cortex of my brain. The computer recognizes me as the picture is transmitted to a memory chip. The mechanism of transmitting the picture to a specific site where it should be recognized is similar in both me and the computer. However, the difference is that I am able to experience the sight of my computer, but the computer is unable to experience me and my essence.

That means I am able to perceive everything with a part of my body that is my brain, but how is it turning all my perceptions and memories in to this conscious self that is me, which I am not able to understand scientifically? I am referring to our inability to locate that part of the brain that ultimately gives rise to the constant thinking process that leads us to experience the world around us. We hypothesize that it is the constant firing of the 1 trillion neuronal cells we have in our brains that's responsible for our thinking process. If that's true, then the computer has thousands of circuits with constant electrical phenomenon going on inside it, but it's not able to think by itself and start experiencing the world around it. It still needs our programming and control. We can say that maybe the computers are not sophisticated enough yet to become alive. So what is this being alive? Is it equal to being able to think and experience? Is the brain solely responsible for it? Then why when we cut off half of the brain in children, do they survive without any problem in their mental or physical functioning? Is the brain functioning as a gateway, a receptacle, or a switchboard to this phenomenon called mind/soul?

It is astonishing. We use our minds every waking moment and sometimes even while we are asleep, but we are oblivious to them most of the time. We are still in the dark about the part of the brain that makes us think, or the thinking process itself. Be it the sum total of firing of 1 trillion neurons and their synapses at the same time or a specific part of it, it is still a mystery.

All these questions remain unanswered with modern-day technologies. I realized we might never be able to find the answers if we continue to address it only by our modern-day, materialistic way of gathering knowledge by testing, retesting, and researching and with hard-core evidence. I realized the answers might lie in going back to our predecessors' way of looking at life and this world.

This thought led me to be in this quest of learning about the human mind. I wanted to know what the ancients thought about this subject. I wanted to know the philosophical and theological perspectives of it. I wanted to compare all this information with modern scientific knowledge and find common grounds.

This book is about that quest.

Tanzia Mustafa, MD
New York

CHAPTER 1

THE ORIGIN OF LIFE

Making sense of our existence in this complex universe has been an everlasting saga of the human race. Century after century has passed, and mankind has moved from caveman status to civilization of the twenty-first century. Most of our knowledge and scientific accomplishments have revolved around our physical, mechanistic, and materialistic perspectives of our existence. We are a race accustomed to believing in something once we see concrete evidence. We like to touch, feel, gather data, test, retest, stratify, screen, measure, analyze, and reproduce the studies. Then we tend to reach a conclusion, which is very easy to accomplish with the physical materials of our everyday reality. However, doing research with an abstract concept like the mind and its processes is very difficult.

I won't deny that we have achieved some progress in behavioral research, which is the outcome of mental processes, but it's not the same when we do research on any other organ of the body with hard-core evidence. As

a result, our progress has been the slowest. We are con-
quering Mars. We are prolonging lives with state-of-the-art
medical technology. We are able to communicate with one
another faster than the speed of light, and so on and so
forth. The question is, then, why we are seeing man-made
disasters, wars, and mass killings? Our planet is in peril due
to our materialistic, mechanistic approach to our existence.

Modern science defines *mind* as a "subjectively perceived, functional entity, based ultimately upon physiological processes but has complex processes of its
own; it governs the total organism and its interaction
with the environment" (Kaplan and Sadock Volume I).
Based on this definition, we have to acknowledge that
the tiniest bacteria, whatever rudimentary brain material
they possess, have a mind that helps them navigate to
their desired food sources and reproduce when they
can. When we add this new paradigm to the animal and
plant kingdoms, the whole equation—our perception of
the whole world—destabilizes. We convince ourselves
that the evolutionary changes we see occurring in nature are all because of natural selection. The organism
has no will in this process. But we are forgetting a step
in that process—the one where the organism has the
ability to process the adversities of its environment with
its rudimentary mind and then tries to change by introducing new genomic changes into its core. This leads to

transcription of information, which leads to translation and production of amino acids, which leads to production of new protein. This leads to a new characteristic of that organism, which leads to better survival.

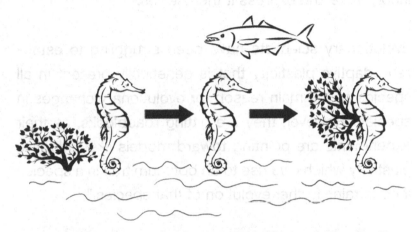

Seahorse absorbing environmental information with its mind. It realizes it can fool the predator if it takes on the shape and color of its environment. Then a few generations after this intent is transmitted to its cellular genomic level leading to new codes in its gene, which converts in to new protein and we see a seahorse with beautiful branches and leaves.

If we look at any aspect of nature, we see there are mental processes in action in every moment. We see birds flying in the sky in certain directions. The birds see, hear, and process information from their environment and act when the time is right. If we search the Internet, we see home videos of house pets and other animal videos. It's amazing how smart these animals are. I remember my first visit to SeaWorld. The killer whales' ability to respond to their trainers was mind-boggling to me.

We see this process everywhere in nature. The ability of insects to camouflage according to their surroundings tells us they have active mental processes that allow them to absorb the environmental information and then incorporate and express it themselves.

Evolutionary scientists have been struggling to establish adaptive plasticity that is genetically present in all species as the main reason for evolutionary changes in species. However, they are hitting roadblocks, as their experiments are pointing toward models like "adaptive plasticity which give rise to an optimum trait in a species it constrains further evolution of that species."

> Empirical studies of adaptive evolution reveal that adaptations to new environments rarely involves single trait, but rather suites of traits that responds to diverse selection pressures. At the whole organism level new environments likely to result in a combination of adaptive and non-adaptive plasticity in a suite of traits, but the consequences of such responses for evolution on ecological time scales remains unexplored territory. (Reznick and CK Ghalambor, et al, 2001)

English naturalist Charles Darwin published *The Origin of Species* in 1859. Almost two hundred years later, we still don't know what to make of his theory. We see organisms, especially aquatic in origin, change their characteristics based on their environments in a short period of time. Trinidad guppies have been used in evolutionary research. They have genetic changes after a few generations when exposed to environmental stress. Through our own observations, we see fish taking the color of coral to fool predators. Insects take on the colors of their environment to fool predators. However, we do not yet have any proof of organisms transitioning into a different species altogether, even in those species under extreme environmental stress and on the verge of extinction. We do not see viruses converting into bacteria or bacteria into amoebas and so on and so forth. Yes, they become resistant to antibiotics and virulent, as in the case of the influenza virus year after year, which is why we have to get an annual flu vaccine. But at its core, it remains the influenza virus.

This gives rise to questions as to whether the evolutionary changes we observe in nature are evolutionary at all. It looks like the species are just trying to fit into the environment to better themselves. They are not trying to evolve into a new species.

When we reduce ourselves to originating from a cell that happened to assemble itself in the primordial water and evolved to become a multicellular organism and then a fish and then an amphibian and so on and so forth till we became *Homo sapiens*, the above-mentioned disasters await the human race. Human beings by nature like to relate to people who are better than us. When we do the opposite and relate to inferior minds, like animals, we behave like them as well. And who knows better than we how we can sometimes act worse than animals, killing others for material gain?

For argument's sake, if we believe that the self-assembled unicellular organism was the origin of life on this planet, according to the definition of *mind*, it has to have a rudimentary mind as well. This is another layer of complexity of living organisms. If we look at a unicellular organism like bacteria at the microscopic level, the complexity of this one-cellular unit is mind-boggling. Just that one cell may possess deadly toxins that produce diseases resulting in death to another living organism. Now if we add mental components to living things, we have a huge problem to address. As per the theory of evolution, nature selects us to change our genetics and evolve into a different species, as this planet is about survival of the fittest. If we consider that mental evolution happened alongside physical evolution of the plant and animal kingdoms, we would see one animal smarter than the other. But what we see is that their intellect is exactly right for themselves. As ethologist Frans de Waal says, "Animals have the brain they need—nothing more, nothing less." A blind and deaf bat is completely capable to survive and reproduce. A lion's intellect is not greater than a tiger's. Our brain structure, which also correlates with our mind, became more and more complicated— not necessarily to survive the harshness of the nature, but rather to acquire knowledge and the ability to love and sacrifice.

If the motivation for the physical evolution of species to species was to survive the harshness of nature, the mental evolution that we notice in higher mammals does not follow the same concept. It actually follows the opposite—that is, to sacrifice, love, nurture, and protect their young. Frans de Waal in his work on primates has established that primates are capable of experiencing humanlike empathy, compassion, and group consciousness. Some species even sacrifice themselves for the cause of the group. If we look at the basic concept of the theory of physical evolution, we see that it completely contradicts the mental evolution in nature. It is as if they are going in two different directions. It also contradicts the Darwinian concept of creating species that are less and less vulnerable and independent. Why would evolution, if it really happened, give rise to a human infant, who is the most vulnerable thing on this planet for a prolonged period of time?

Why are we giving so much power to nature? Are we not substituting God? This substitution follows the same concept of our mental makeup, as we can see and somehow quantify nature so we can relate to it to some extent. We cannot see and fathom God, so He is out of the question. However, we are attributing some mental processes to nature to that of a mad scientist, who randomly produces species after species with directional selection and has the ability to discard the genotypes that are not fit for survival. But we are not doing a good job so far in understanding this mad scientist.

If we rewrite the theory of evolution with the knowledge of mind and incorporate it into the physical body of a species, we also have to acknowledge the mental evolution of a species and mental competition on an ongoing basis. In reality, we see the animal kingdom is content with its qualities. It tries to better itself at times to fool predators, but it is not in competition with itself.

We only see mental evolution in the human mind, as well as mental competition. No other animal can come close to the mental capacity of *Homo sapiens*. If we consider that Cro-Magnon man was the first *Homo sapiens* who roamed this earth fifty thousand years ago, we have come a long way in terms of our mental evolution, but not so much in our physical characteristics. Most importantly, we did not become completely different a species, although we have dealt with nature's trials and tribulations.

We share genetic and physical characteristics being earthlings with our fellow earthlings, the plants and the animals. We share the experience of being alive. We feel pain and pleasure in some extent in similar ways. A squirrel needs to be distractible and has to react in a moment's notice. The ADHD they have is their norm. All of us are unique and special in our own ways. Our sharing of some basic building blocks of existence does not qualify us to think our origin is from the same unicellular organism.

The difference of being a human is that we possess creativity, vision, compassion, and will, which are unique to only our species. Our mental capacities surpass all the intellects the animal and plant kingdom share together.

It's time we need to acknowledge our true potential. Instead of looking down, it's time to look up and align ourselves with our true nature.

Let's delve deeper into the mechanics.

CHAPTER 2

THE REALM OF PHILOSOPHY

Every culture, every tribe gave birth to those wise men who devoted their lives to acquire knowledge and guide their tribes with their wisdom. They were not published or known by the rest of the world, but common people used their wisdom in their everyday lives. Even Socrates's work was never published. He was introduced to the world by his student Plato after his death. I would like to pay tribute to those philosophers who made my ancestors lives easier by their sayings, fables, poems, and songs.

Lalon Shah and Hasan Raja were two mystics born in Bengal province in undivided India. Their wisdom has been transmitted through their poetry and songs, sung and recited by common people even now in rural Bengal. Khana was another example of a visionary whose fables and sayings are still practiced in rural Bengal. Her sayings are titled *Khanar bachan*.

I did not want to miss this opportunity to acknowledge their work, which inspired me and still does.

In this chapter I will mostly talk about the philosophers—the famous ones who tried to conceptualize the mind in their work.

Milesians

History of philosophy begins with Milesians. Miletus was an Ionian city on the Mediterranean shore, what is now Turkey. Among the Milesians, Thales and his students Anaximander and Anaximenes are the most prominent ones. They were known for hypothesizing that everything has a source, and the source is the primordial water. In 585 BC, these wise men of old were grappling to connect everything they saw in nature with each other. They had their views about earth and its elements, their cosmological views, and their views of mind, or soul. They were also called natural philosophers, as their work mostly revolved around the naturalistic phenomenon.

Thales was able to observe natural phenomenon like eclipses and was able to forecast about future corps. His student Anaximander first drew a world map with circuits. Their cosmological view was that everything originates from the same source, and everything possesses a soul. To Thales and his students, soul or mind was something Kinetic, and they believed magnesium stone has a soul because it moves iron. Thales also thought souls are intermingled in the universe, for which he thought all things are full of gods. Thales said the mind of the world is God. The sum of the things is be-souled and full of spirits. In other words, they believed everything in this universe has some sort of mind in it.

Pythagoras and Pythagoreanism

Pythagoras was born on the Island of Samos in Greece before the middle of the sixth century. As a young man he migrated to Italy and found his Pythagorean society. Although the Ionian tradition was materialistic, it sought explanation in such sensible opposites as the hot and cold, wet and dry—characters proper to perceptions. On the contrary, Pythagoras sought explanation in the form of structure and form—a form in essence, numerical. Pythagoreans assumed that the world is a Harmonia, an orderly and proportionate adjustment of parts within a complex whole.

We all know the contributions of Pythagorean concepts in geometry and mathematics. Our scope here is to understand their concept of soul/mind/higher mind. Pythagoreans believed the soul is immortal and sub-scribed to the Egyptian concept of reincarnation as an-imals and practiced abstention from all forms of meat. Pythagoras founded a cult society with religious taboos.

It was understood as a way of life whose aim was purification of soul and its release from the prison of the body. Salvation (release from the wheel of rebirth) was to be attained by understanding the beauty and order of the cosmos, especially shown in the circles of heavens and reproducing that order in one's soul. Philosophy then is the purification or catharsis of the soul. According to Pythagoreans, philosophy (love of wisdom or knowledge) is a regimen to free the soul from the burden of sense and corruption of physicality and materialistic perspectives of everyday life. Pythagoreans devoted their lives to mathematics and tried to explain world order in mathematical terms. However, they published little partly because of its character as a cult society and emphasis on secrecy.

The Pluralists

Two philosophers, Empedocles and Anaxagoras, attempted to give a description of mind. According to Pluralists, the mind is infinite, self-ruled, and mixed with nothing, for it is the finest of everything and the purest. It has knowledge about everything and the greatest power. Mind controls everything—both the greater and smaller that have life. They continued the Milesians' concept that everything has a mind be it alive or an inanimate object.

Socrates and Plato

Socrates was born in Athens in 469 BC. He did not publish any literature. His wisdom was mostly practiced and
taught verbally. He would strike a conversation with a
fellow or a stranger, which would lead to a discussion,
and in the end, both parties will clarify their understanding of a subject. Socrates was a mysterious man. It is
upon Plato's portrait of him that we chiefly rely on for
information.

Inscribed in the temple at Delphi were the words of
Apollo: "Know thyself." Before Socrates, this inscription
was understood as to know one's social status. The
peasant should not behave like the king, and the king
should not behave like the gods. Socrates transformed
this injunction by turning it inward. The true aim of life, as
Plato put it in The *Apology of Socrates*, is to "make one's
soul as good as possible." Human happiness consists of
spiritual perfection, and spiritual perfection implies and
is implied by self-knowledge. The claim of morality on
a man is ultimately the claim of his own human nature
on itself; only when a man is able to understand himself
clearly will he be able to discern good from evil. It is for
this reason that "an unexamined life is not worth living."
As a moral teacher, Socrates was peculiar in that he did
not preach, but questioned, always wearing a mask of

ignorance. It appears "know thyself" was the cry of humanity in its everlasting saga of finding its place in this universe.

Plato

Plato was born in Athens in a distinguished Athenian parentage in 428 BC. He was in touch with Socrates as a very young man. When Socrates was put to death in 399 BC, Plato undertook to justify his memory and carry on his work by writing a series of dialogues. *The Apology* and *Euthyphro* belong to this group of dialogues.

The work of Plato mostly dealt with ethics. Plato's view of reality is that there are two worlds—a world of opinions and the world of knowledge, which is the real one. The contents of the world of knowledge are forms—divine and immaterial and fully intelligible, such as justice, goodness, and equality, which can only be apprehended by reason. The world of opinion is not fully real, and it is not fully unreal either. Its contents are the changing particulars of the material world. Plato undertook to solve— in a literal sense, the material world was made the seal and symbol of the intelligible. The moral ideal for men was to attain to knowledge, thereby introducing the beauty and order of the divine in to their own souls and hopefully to society as well.

Aristotle

Aristotle was the first scientist and someone to whom all the scientists in the world are indebted. He created the foundations for all the branches of biology. The era when knowledge of the external world, both living and nonliving, as well as astronomy and mathematics was practiced as a mishmash, he brought order and structure to them. He founded the concepts of botany, zoology, physics, and metaphysics. Surprisingly, his observations on mental processes are still valid and accurate in the twenty-first century.

He had three books written on the subject of the soul/mind. Aristotle's *De Anima*, meaning "on the soul," is about all living things possessing a soul/mind of different kinds. Some commentators have suggested that Aristotle's term *soul* is better translated as "life force." Now the question arises what is a life force? Where does it reside? Is it in the vital organs of the body, like the heart and lungs or in the brain? Or is it somewhere else? Even now, many hundreds of years later, we still do not know the answer. Aristotle believed that the soul is the form of, or essence, of any living thing. It is not a distinct substance from the body that it is in. It is the possession of a soul (of a specific kind) that makes an organism an organism at all. Thus the notion of a body without a soul or of a soul in the wrong kind of body is simply unintelligible.

Aristotle did not subscribe to the concept of reincarnation like some of his predecessors.

His treaties were divided in to three books. The first book introduces the theme of the treaties and provides a survey of Aristotle's predecessors' views about the soul. The second book outlines his definition of soul/mind and his studies about it. It discusses nutrition and reproduction, as well as all the modalities of perceptions all the living things possess. He discusses all the five sense. He also recognizes that some animals have some special senses, including memory and imagination.

Book three discusses the mind or rational soul itself, which belongs to humans alone. He argues that thinking is different than both the sense of perception and imagination. His argument is that senses can never lie, and imagination is a power to make something sensed earlier appear again. While thinking can sometimes be false, he postulated that the mind should be considered to have two faculties; one contains all the ideas, and one executes the ideas in action.

He began his treaties by conceding that attempting to define the mind/soul is one of the most difficult questions in the world, and after hundreds of years, it still remains the same.

Perhaps the most important but obscure argument in the whole book is Aristotle's demonstration of the immortality of the *thinking* part of the human mind. He argues that because the mind acts with no bodily organ, it exists without the body. And if it exists apart from the matter, it cannot be corrupted or die; therefore, the human mind is immortal.

René Descartes

René Descartes acquired the status of one of the canonical philosophical writers of the early modern period. He joined the ranks of Aristotle, Thomas Aquinas, and subsequently David Hume, Immanuel Kant, and Georg Wilhelm Friedrich Hegel as foremost among Western philosophers who have helped shaped the way in which we currently think about the nature and limits of human understanding. Descartes defended the competence of human understanding to explain the natural world and who provided the methodological and metaphysical foundations that underpinned what we now call scientific knowledge.

He was born in central France in 1596. Apart from intermittent brief travels, he spent most of his life in the Netherlands. In 1619 he conceived a project for renewal and unifications of the sciences. Following some travel, he settled in the Netherlands. However, he wanted to keep his privacy and changed residences and did not publish for twenty years while thinking, meditating, and writing. Most of his famous works were published in the last ten years of his life. He addressed many of the issues upper-most in the minds of his contemporaries. He explicitly confronted the challenges raised by a form of skepticism that had become endemic in European intellectual circles. Skepticism that said all our beliefs are more or less doubt-ful was widely discussed for at least hundred years be-fore Descartes published *Meditations of First Philosophy.* According to his theory, human beings are composed completely of two distinct kinds of substances—matter and mind. Mind is defined by the ability to think, and mat-ter is defined in terms of extension in three dimensions. This concept of mind is also known as Cartesian dualism.

Once he embarked on this project, Descartes pre-sented a traditional picture of the soul as a spiritual or nonphysical substance that is inexplicably united with a body that functions like a biological machine. He hy-pothesized there are very narrow tubes through which an extremely subtle matter flows. He called that sub-tle matter "animal spirits," which he believed carried messages to and from the brain in both directions.

One of the central features of the Cartesian enterprise was confidence in the powers of human understanding and his challenge against skepticism that the human mind cannot perceive anything with certainty. He postulated that reason alone should stand in judgment on all human opinions and not just related to faith.

The first meditation in his writing discusses the distinction of the human soul and the body, as well as God's existence. The second meditation discusses the nature and processes of the human mind and comes to a conclusion that "I am therefore precisely a thinking thing, that is a mind, soul, intellect or reason. I am a genuine thing and I truly exist because I think."

Descartes's mission was to establish the essence of life or the life force, which he postulated was our ability to think. We have proof to this claim today. We know we can lose the functions of many parts of our brain and body due to diseases like ALS (also known as Lou Gehrig's disease); however, we continue to exist due to our ability to think. Stephen Hawking is an example of a functioning mind with a nonfunctioning body and brain.

Immanuel Kant (1724–1804)

A German philosopher and a central figure in modern philosophy, Kant argued that fundamental concepts structure human experience and that reason is the source of morality. He attempted to explain the relationship between reason and human experiences while resisting the skepticism of thinkers like David Hume. Kant argued that our experiences depend on necessary features of our minds. Among other things, Kant believed that the concepts of space and time are integral parts of the brain and mind, and so is cause and effect, which we can prove with our twenty-first century knowledge of neurological science. We know that when certain parts of brain are dysfunctional, the mind loses the sense of time, and with other lesions, the mind loses the sense of space. However, Kant's stance as a rationalist was that all knowledge does not come from just our external experience, but rather is a combination of our prior innate ideas (or a priori knowledge) and our current experiences. This was a paradigm shift in the world of philosophy. He influenced many thinkers in Germany and other parts of the world, and he moved philosophy beyond the debate between the rationalists and empiricists.

The external world, he wrote, provides those things that we sense. But it is our minds that process this information and give it order, allowing us to comprehend it. The mind supplies the conditions of space and time to experience objects. Without the concepts, perceptions are nondescript; without the perceptions, concepts are meaningless. Thus the famous statement: "Thoughts without content are empty, intuitions (perceptions) without concepts are blind."

Summary

The following facts emerges from this discussion;

1. Milesians, the most ancient philosophers, believed that everything originated from the same source and has its own mind, which is the core substance of any material, whether living or nonliving.

2. Subsequently, philosophers started focusing on their own makeup and became cognizant that "know thyself" is the key to understand both the internal and external processes of the world. As a result, they started to work on ethics, morality, metaphysics, and, last but not the least, the human mind.

3. Aristotle, the father of science, made a solid foundation for the next generations to work on his concepts and processes of mental functioning.

4. Descartes elaborated on Aristotle's thoughts and defended the human mind's competence from the skepticism and provided a dual concept of mind and body, namely dualism. He also postulated that the core essence of being alive is our ability to think—hence, the phrase, "I think, so I exist."

5. Immanuel Kant was the pioneer rationalist who refuted the empiricist ideas that everything we learn is from our external experiences. He postulated that we have a priori knowledge/programming in our brains, which is innate—for example, our sense of time and space, as well as our sense of cause and effect.

CHAPTER 3

REALM OF RELIGIONS

Religion can be defined as the way humans attempt to understand and interact with their world to give meaning to their lives. Another dictionary defines religion as "the expression of man's belief and reverence for a superhuman power recognized as the creator and governor of the universe." The history of religion is as old as the history of man himself. The *New Encyclopedia Britannica* says, "as far as scholars have discovered, there has never existed any people, anywhere, at any time who were not in some sense religious." On the other hand, certainly world history must give us pause and cause us to wonder what role religion has played in the many wars that have devastated mankind and caused untold sufferings. Why have so many people been killed and continue to be killed in the name of religion? The Crusades, the Inquisition, the ongoing Middle East conflicts, al-Qaida, ISIS, the Hindu-Muslim clashes in India—all these events certainly make us wonder if we really need religion in our lives. Blaise Pascal said, "Men never do evil so completely and cheerfully as when they do it from religious conviction." Does religion actually serve any purpose for human nature?

To answer that question, we need to delve in to the history of human behaviors. We see there has always been a need for the human mind to relate with a superpower, be it in the form mythological god and goddess, nature, or in modern technological advances. We can also refer to our film industry, which is cashing in on our unconscious need to be saved by a hero like Batman or Superman. The same unconscious need in ancient times manifested in having a human avatar, prophets, or saints. Time and time again, thousands of religious leaders and prophets have formulated their religions and catered to the need of the population.

If we dig deeper in human psychology and discuss theories like object relations or self-psychology, we see that from infancy we are programmed to be nurtured and to build a relationship with a power who is superior to us (our mothers). We then learn, and from the interactions with her, we are equipped so that an independent human emerges. A human infant has to be dependent on its caretaker for an extra-long period, which is not seen in any other species in nature. This programming—or, as Kant says, a priori knowledge—might be the reason humans are almost compelled to relate with a superpower. This is also a unique phenomenon only in humans. However, if we think the need to relate with a superior power ends when we become adults, then we are wrong. We continue to have that need, which manifests as our faith in God; otherwise, we substitute it by having faith in our life partners, nature, or our faith in science and technology.

We can ask questions like: Why is the human infant the most vulnerable creature on this planet? Even a baby bacteria is equipped to take care of itself right after it is born, unlike a human infant who takes many years of nurturance to be self-sufficient. This prolonged dependence and need for nurturance sure is a priori knowledge, as Kant explained, and contributes to our sense of being cut off from an infinite power source.

To fulfill that need, philosophers had postulated their visions of a superpower from time to time. Then there were other visionaries who proclaimed themselves as prophets of God and tried to guide humankind. If we look closely, these wise men of old are doing similar work—that is, trying to find the truth. However, one group is claiming that they are being connected by the superpower himself, and the other group is not. If we look closely, we can see that their methods of coming to a hypothesis involves years doing of meditation, being in seclusion, and being in strife, even losing their lives in that process. Like Socrates, Galileo was executed, and we know how the lives of Abraham, Moses, and Jesus evolved. I have discussed how Descartes took twenty years to publish his first meditation. However, the group who claimed to be the prophets of God were mostly illiterate and had a hard time preserving their teachings in scriptures and dealt with adversities of their time and from their people.

The point I am trying to make here is that our innate programming of searching for a superpower had given rise to many religions and mythology, and we have a myriad of religions being practiced in this planet. When we go for questioning the other religions' authenticity and look down on the practitioners of other religions, which most religions forbid, then we see the wars, fights, and religious battles. The fights and wars are not the religion's fault. They are the failure of the practitioners to practice the religion right. Religions are laws and structure. As we know, laws vary from country to country, region to region. The same is true with religions. However, the ultimate goal for any law and any religion is to benefit humanity.

If we look at biblical genealogy starting from Adam, there are many prophets who proclaimed that they received guidance from God. According to Koranic teachings, there were 124,000 prophets sent to mankind over time to guide the human race. My job here is not to question the authenticity of those religions but to find the common foundations regarding what all those belief systems have to say about mind and mental processes.

It is very difficult to tweak information about mind when all the teachings of major religions were addressed toward man's mind rather than the body. It was an automatic process for man to comprehend, preach, and learn by his mind but be completely oblivious about the process that was involved. However, we find mentioning of soul/mind in each and every religion, and most of them declare it to be immortal. If we look at Hinduism, even the religion has evolved from Pre-Vedic era when the religion was dominated by animistic beliefs and an extensive world of demons and evil spirits, compared to the Post-Vedic era when a new religion began to address humans' ability to take charge of their own lives and decrease the importance of gods in their lives. A sacred power called Brahman is the source of existence and atman (soul) in all things, and people were introduced to four books of Vedas. According to Hindu philosophy, Brahman and the atman prevailed and sustained life. Hinduism encourages detachment from materialism and prescribes regular practice of yoga to tap into the infinite power of Brahman and atman, which is the psychophysical exercise known in the West as meditation. Although there are

Hindu writings about states of consciousness, identity, and motivation, there is no detailed description of mental processes. Hindu philosophy recognizes the two different parts of mind as the lower mind and the higher mind, Vivek or conscience. In Hinduism, vivek means wisdom or knowledge which is only given to human, which makes human completely different from animals and plants.

The three monotheistic religions, namely Judaism, Christianity, and Islam, have multiple commonalities in terms of the concept of mind. Sigmund Freud, being a Jewish neurologist and formulating a structural division of mind, implied he had his religious influences conceptualizing those theories. Freud had conceptualized the mind having three distinct parts: id, ego, and superego. Id represents the lower mind, which makes sure the individual's selfish needs are being met. Ego is that part of the mind that is always negotiating and balancing one's needs versus the collective needs. Superego is the part of mind that functions as the conscience of the individual.

Koranic teaching states humans and all creation are created from God's *nur*, which means light. This means the core substance of anything is God's light. It also recognizes the human mind as having two parts. *Nafs*, the lower mind, is responsible for selfish actions and is the part of the mind vulnerable to be influenced by Satan.

The higher mind, the conscience, is less vulnerable. So any action that is perpetuated by the *nafs* may involve wrong judgment. However, the conscience invoking judgment or actions is more plausible.

The question is, how are we be able to identify these two different parts of our minds and apply them to our everyday decisions, and what is the scientific basis of it? I will discuss this in detail if the next chapters. The Koran distinctively describes the human mind and body to be in two different domains. The body resides in the realm of Khalq, or material plane, and the mind resides in the domain of Amar, or the plane of spirits. In Islamic culture, emotional responses like extreme anger, extreme sadness, and extreme happiness were always discouraged. There are practices outlined to control extremes of emotion. Alcohol and mind-altering substances are prohibited, as they can alter emotional states and one's judgment.

All three major monotheistic religions are putting their emphasis on faith or belief—essentially, faith in God and his prophets. I want to elaborate on the word *faith*. In psychiatric terms, faith/belief is a strong mental attribute that is unshakable or set in stone. I would like to give an example of strong faith. Suppose you caught someone stealing, and you wanted him to go through a lie detector test. Two people will pass the lie detector test—that is, their blood pressure and pulse will not fluctuate. One of these people is a sociopath who developed a strong faith in himself that everything he does is right—even stealing. So his mental and physical makeup are aligned, and there is no conflict between his id and superego. The other one is someone with a psychiatric illness completely detached with reality. The rest of us would be conflicted, as we have some sense of right and wrong, and would not pass the lie detector test. To have any type of faith or strong belief, it has to change the whole makeup of you, even your internal autonomic nervous system. All monotheistic religions emphasize this type of unshakable faith in God. In other words, the *certitude* or *faith* is attained by a human mind being convinced in all different levels of conscious thinking.

The implications of a belief system are very broad and complex. In psychiatric terms, a fixed false belief is a delusion and a mental illness. However, a belief system grounded in reality, appropriate action, and hard work can work as a foundation for success as the faith associated with vision and creativity. That's why we see people with faith in themselves attaining superhuman goals.

All three monotheistic religions have a concept of Satan or the devil. Satan's demonic influence was attributed to Jews, Romans, gentiles, and dissident Christians.

As per Islamic literature, Satan is a being, mostly working form the realm of Amar, and has power to influence the human mind. Many verses in the Koran teach to clear one's thinking from the influence of Satan and be able to have clear judgment. The part of mind it influences mostly is the *nafs*, or the lower mind.

I have explored Buddhism, Confucianism, and Zoroastrianism. Although Buddhism has tremendous influence on Western psychotherapies, hypnosis, and meditation, descriptive literature is hard to find about the exact mental processes how to achieve a state of meditation, such as which part of mind is at work, etc.

Summary

1. All three monotheistic religions have many common concepts about mental processes. Although Sigmund Freud popularized the structural divisions of the mind as id, ego, and superego, it was already known to practitioners of all three monotheistic religions.

2. Koranic teachings favor Descartes' dualism.

3. Most of the religions of the world conceptualize a devil's presence. Koranic teaching specifies the lower mind (*nafs*) to be the most vulnerable for satanic influence.

4. Common characteristics between religions like Buddhism and Catholicism, Islam and Judaism, and basic concepts like the soul/mind being immortal, etc. implies that there was a common pool from which each religion drew its basic beliefs. Is that common source the higher mind/God?

CHAPTER 4

MODERN SCIENCE AND MIND

In this chapter my goal is to give an overview of the brain and mind in simplistic terms in light of modern science. I will discuss a little bit of anatomy, as well as physiology of the brain and its functions initially. Later I will try to discern the mental functions and correlate the functions with different parts of the brain.

Although the brain is the organ we refer to for neurological functions, as well as mental functioning, sometimes it is very difficult to discern the line demarcating these two fields. The best way to solve this problem would be if we consider that the brain is the organ of the body that performs certain functions. Then we can delineate the functions that are under the domain of neurology and the functions that are under psychiatric or mental domain.

The functions of the brain under neurological domain are roughly as follows: motor movements of our extremities, including the body, face, and spine; all the perceptual modalities, such as vision, audition, tactile sensation, taste, and smell. Language, spatial sense, sense of time, writing, and reading are neurological functions as well.

Being able to experience and feel a myriad of emotions are psychiatric, or mental, functions of the brain. Being able to perform cognitive functions, such as attention, concentration, memorization, information processing, social cognition, think, judgment, and impulse control are functions that fall under psychiatric domain. As you can see, the abstract functions are under the domain of psychiatry, and the functions of the brain that are quantifiable are under the domain of neurology. It's like a computer's hard wiring and its soft wiring. There are numerous overlapping of functions exists, as you can imagine, that we designate to field of neuropsychiatry.

Following is some anatomical information about the brain:

The building blocks of the brain are called neurons. A neuron is a cell that has a body and an elongated projection that transmits electrical impulses from one neuron to another. The brain consists of 100 billion neuronal cells. These cells are connected to each other in places called synapses, which function as a docking station. The neuronal cells are linked together by a combined chemical and electrical communication system. The chemicals that are released in a synapse from one neuron can lead to a cascade of chemical and electrical events in the other neurons meeting in the synapse. Some of these reactions might increase the electrical voltage inside the cell, and some will decrease the voltage, resulting in signal transmission to other neurons and eventually leading to a specific action of the human body, such as blinking an eye muscle or the mere act of seeing something. An average neuron is connected to about 10,000 other neurons at a synaptic junction with hundreds of trillions of connections among a web like neural network. There are countless combinations of possible activation profiles. The term *neural net profile* is used to describe a certain pattern of activation of the complex layers of neuronal circuits. These complex layers of neuronal circuits are grouped.

Anatomically, the brain is divided in to multiple regions. Broadly, the brain is divided in to two hemispheres—the left and right brain—connected by a group of insulated neurons called insula. Each hemisphere is divided into multiple lobes: frontal lobes, parietal lobes, temporal lobes, occipital lobes, hippocampus or limbic system, amygdala, thalamus, hypothalamus, midbrain, and brain stem. Each of these lobes is identifiable with certain functions of the brain.

Roughly, the following functions are assigned to different regions of the brain, although more and more research indicates the brain functions in unison rather than in a split way.

Frontal lobes are known as performing the executive functions of human brain. The executive functions include planning, setting goals, information processing, assessing ones' circumstances, etc. Parietal lobes are associated with motor movements and sensory functions of the body. They are also responsible for our spatial sense and timing. Temporal lobes perform language function in reading and writing form. They also have the auditory cortex, which is associated with our ability to hear. Occipital lobes have our visual cortex where our visual stimuli are processed and we are able to experience sight. The hippocampus or limbic system is the inner part of brain situated deep and is responsible for emotional responses. Thalamus is a relay station and responsible for experiencing pain sensation. Hypothalamus is situated just below thalamus and functions as the control room for all the different hormones we have in our bodies, like growth hormone, thyroid hormone, male and female hormones, etc. The midbrain and brain stem are the place all the basic life support systems are situated. This is where the respiratory center, cardiac center, consciousness, sleep, and wakefulness centers are situated. The midbrain and brain stem are also the production sites for neurotransmitters, dopamine, serotonin, etc.

If we compare brains of animals with the human brain, there are many distinctions present. We see reptilians have only a brain stem and midbrain situated in the base of the brain. Birds and mammals have a limbic system in addition to their brain stem and midbrain. That's why we see phenomenon of attachment with their offspring in birds and mammals, although only for a short period of time. This is mostly absent in reptiles and in amphibians.

The neocortex is the surrounding layer of neuronal cells that covers the deeper structures such as the brain stem, midbrain, thalamus, and hypothalamus mentioned above. The neocortex ultimately gives rise to areas like the frontal lobe, temporal lobe, etc. All mammals possess a neocortex. The human neocortex is two hundred times larger than the phylogenetically early mammals. The overall increase in human cortex comes primarily from marked increase in surface area rather than cortical thickness. The average surface area of human brain is three and a half times larger than that of the orangutan. Moreover, the human brain continues to develop newer circuits, especially in frontal and parietal lobes of the brain, until the third decade of life. In contrast, the corresponding structures of brains in chimpanzees and other higher primates reach comparable levels of maturity by the second and third year of life.

Earlier we touched upon how the electrical impulses are generated in the neurons and how they are transmitted. Now I'll discuss a little bit about neurotransmitters and their receptors. There are multiple neurotransmitters that are being produced, namely dopamine, serotonin, acetylcholine, nicotine, and endorphins, which are opioid substance to control pain. These are the prominent ones. These neurotransmitters are responsible for many different functions; however, we will refer to them for mediation of emotional balance at this time. These neurotransmitters are chemical substances produced in certain production sites in the brain, and depending on their scarcity and availability or presence in excessive amounts, our mood, thinking, coordination of movements, and pain sensation can be altered. The neurotransmitters are usually produced inside the cell body, secreted in the synapse, and eventually attach to specific receptors, which ultimately can change the action potential inside the neuronal cell or even induce different changes in cellular functions, including protein synthesis, changes in cell membrane, resting potentials, etc.

However, more and more scientists are becoming aware that there are functional processes present in the brain that we are unaware of at this time other than neurotransmitter release and electrical impulse transmission.

In short, that was a brief overview of the anatomy and physiology of the brain.

Let's discuss mind in terms of modern science.

Definition of the mind according to modern science:

A generally accepted view of the mind is that it emanates from a portion of the activity of the brain. According to Kaplan and Sadock's basic Ideas of mind,

The mind is a processor of energy and information. Energy is contained within the activations of neural circuits. However, the mind is much more than some outcome of energy flow. The mind is considered as a subjectively perceived functional entity, based ultimately upon physical processes but with complex processes of its own. It governs the total organism and its interaction with the environment.

This definition describes the mind coming from inside out. All the neurological and physiological processes give rise to the phenomenon called the mind, which governs the whole organism.

As you may have noticed, the mind is still a subjective process. We cannot yet objectively say that this electrical wave in the electroencephalogram is the representative of an active mental process or this dopamine-serotonin combination is the result of our thinking process. Based on the functions of mind I mentioned earlier, if we look at it outside in, we can come up with a figure like this:

Thinking process/mind/spirit/ soul (or primary mental level)

Being informed by different parts of the brain (or secondary brain level)

1. Frontal lobes allow us to be attentive, plan, and judge our circumstances.

2. Parietal lobes allow us to do or sensory and motor functions.

3. Temporal lobes enable us to use our language skills.

4. The limbic system colors our thinking with different types of emotions.

5. Midbrain and the brain stem keep us conscious, awake, and alert.

6. The neurotransmitters and their receptors affect our mood and perception of our outside world.

In Michael Jackson's "Billy Jean" music video, while he is moonwalking, for every step he takes, a part of the floor lights up. In the same way, the brain lights up part by part when it links with our thinking process. Imagine Michael Jackson is our thinking process, and the floor lighting up is our brain. Although we can see Michael Jackson, we cannot see or explain our thinking process as of yet.

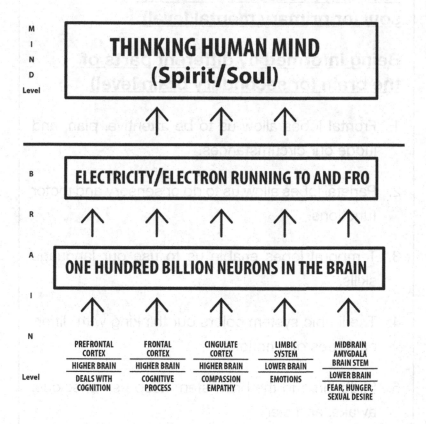

One might question that if we don't know the processes involved in thinking, how are we able to treat all these mental disorders with medications and people are relieved of symptoms?

As we know, most mental disorders occur due to abnormalities in the secondary brain level. In depression, for example, brain neurotransmitters serotonin and dopamine production is reduced, leading to a depressed state of mind that colors one's thinking. Depression medication raises the serotonin level of the brain in the secondary brain level. The other modality is called cognitive behavioral therapy, which addresses the thinking process in the primary level. When done in combination, it leads to a better outcome of the condition.

If we consider dementia a mental condition where the whole brain is atrophied or shrunk in size, we see the person has poor memory and their ability to perform executive functioning is diminished. However, they never lose their ability to think. The pathology of dementia lies mostly in the prefrontal cortex of the brain, and the neurotransmitter acetylcholine is associated with dementia. In Lou Gehrig's disease, although the person's brain becomes nonfunctional, as well as their muscles in the patient's body, the person remains cognitively aware and the ability to think remains intact more or less. In mania, we see the thinking process is accelerated due to excessive presence of stimulatory neurotransmitter, so when

we prescribe medication to suppress the excessive production of neurotransmitter, the mania subsides.

Sigmund Freud and the Models of the Mind

Sigmund Freud was a neurologist (1856–1939) who strived
to describe mind and its processes. He conceptualized a
topographical model of the mind initially and categorized
it on the basis of memory and attention. The parts were
called the conscious, preconscious, and unconscious.
Conscious thinking is referred to what is going on here
and now. Preconscious thinking might involve thinking
in the background that happened a few days ago, and
unconscious refers to some memories which happened
in the remote past.

Then later he wanted to describe the psychic apparatus
structurally. He conceptualized three different parts of
mind—the id, ego, and superego. He stated the id is the
part that is the primitive mind (or primitive thinking process), which makes us aware of our basic selfish needs. It
encompasses our instinctual drives, operates according
to the primary process, and dictates of the pleasure principle. Ego is the intermediate part that mediates between
the id and superego. Ego spans all three topographic
dimensions of conscious, preconscious, and unconscious. Logical and abstract thinking are the domain of

conscious and preconscious parts of mind. However, defense mechanisms reside in the unconscious domain of mind. All motoric and sensory functions and perception are ego functions. In regards to external events, it performs the task by being aware of the stimuli and interacting, adapting, or developing long-standing memories as resources for the future. In terms of internal events, the ego controls the demands of the id or instincts, deciding whether the id should be allowed to get the satisfaction right now, postpone it for a better situation favorable for the external world, or suppress the external stimulation altogether.

Synthesis of Freud's structural and topographical theories of Mind

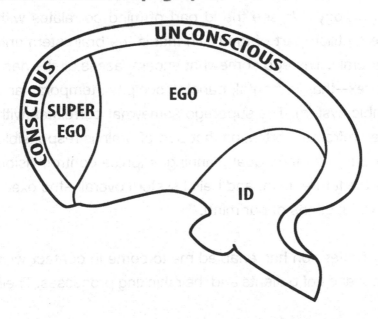

In essence, the ego controls motility, perception, contact with reality through the defense mechanisms available to it, and the delay or modulation of the drive or instincts.

The third component of this tripartite structural model of mind is the superego. The superego establishes and maintains the person's moral conscience on the basis of a complex system of ideals and values internalized from one's parents and the social culture in which a person was born and brought up.

Although we do not have statistically significant evidence of where the id, ego, superego, situated in the brain, we can try to correlate the Freudian structural theory of mind with our current knowledge of brain anatomy and physiology. We see the id part of mind correlates with the reptilian part of the brain that is the brain stem and midbrain. The ego somewhat encompasses all the neo-cortex—that is, frontal, parietal, occipital, temporal, and limbic system. The superego somewhat correlates with the prefrontal cortex, as that part of brain is responsible for our judgment, goal planning, impulse control, vision for the future, faith, and belief system overall—the exec-utive functions of our mind.

My profession has enabled me to come in contact with thousands of patients and their thinking processes. Their ways of experiencing the external world in the light of the internal psychic apparatus. Some made poor judgments and got in to trouble, and some made right decisions and had good outcomes. Before I give some examples, I would like to define thoughts and the thinking process in scientific terms.

There is no universally accepted definition of thoughts. Suggested basic elements include propositions (i.e., functions containing meaning), images, and lexical and semantic symbols. Thought is a cognitive process that can lead to thinking in a parallel fashion even we are not conscious or alert (while asleep). Thought can be expressed through consciousness and language. So we can measure thought and the thinking process only through indirect measure. It was previously thought that it's possible that the functional basis of mental processes such as thinking, feeling, and remembering would somehow be found in individual neurons. It was postulated that the frontal lobe is responsible for cognitive functions of the brain, so thoughts and thinking originate from frontal lobe. However, current research supports integrated actions of many neurons working together. Based on work with hundreds of Russian soldiers who had suffered many brain injuries, Alexander Luria, a Russian scientist, collected data consistent with their brain injuries. He noted that any behavioral or cognitive deficits a soldier suffered due to a specific lesion in the brain was not circumscribed in that specific part of the brain; rather, it had a widespread consequence.

Based on numerous studies like that, we can presume that the thinking process involves all different parts of the brain at the same time. Thought can be generated from the any part of the brain, from an old memory or an active, outside trigger. So thoughts—the essential part of the thinking process—can originate from anywhere in the brain at any time. The environment can be a trigger to a specific kind of thought. If a person has an old trauma associated with noise, the noise might trigger violence or aggression.

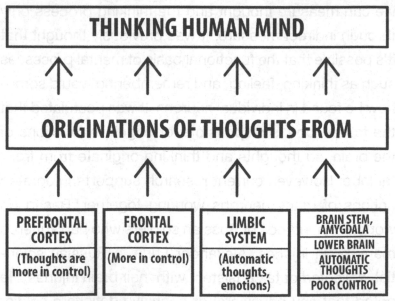

Thoughts can originate from any part of the Brain. Higher the brain location, the more control we have on those throughts. The thoughts produced in the lower and deeper parts of brain are more automatic with poor or no control.

Can we structure and discipline our thoughts, which are both an automatic and voluntary phenomenon? Aaron Beck's cognitive behavioral therapy sheds light on that. As I mentioned, some of our thoughts are automatic and we have poor control over them. These are the thoughts that are being produced from the lower brain—the limbic system, amygdala, midbrain, and brain stem. We can also refer to it as the id. If we analyze the id-associated thoughts, we see these are the thoughts that are generated mostly to preserve our selfish interests. If we are hungry and the hunger center (which is situated in the brain stem) is activated, we will start visualizing food of different varieties.

The higher brain—the ego and superego—will start generating thoughts as well. Suppose we are given an option for a calorie-rich, tasty food versus a well-balanced, moderately tasty food. The higher brain and lower brain will be at war. The lower mind will want the instant gratification, but the higher mind will advocate for a delayed gratification and advocate for the healthy option. However, it is the person's habit versus self-restraint that eventually will win. If we look at this phenomenon, it is an ongoing process with every choice we make in everyday life on a moment-by-moment basis. There is a right and wrong way to perceive a situation and take action for every person.

The thoughts, which are mostly automatic and originate from the id, will lead us to act impulsively, out of fear, and for our instant gratification. When using our judgment and thinking originating from the ego and superego/conscience, our choices might be closer to the right option.

We can hypothesize about these divisions of the mind and the thinking processes. However, being able to discern these thoughts of origin and take control of them by the higher centers is the real battle. Based on these concepts, different modalities of psychotherapies are administered. Freud conceptualized psychodynamic psychotherapy, Aaron Beck created the foundation of cognitive behavioral therapy, and Socrates followed the motto of "know thyself." Because thoughts are intertwined with our everyday experiences, our thoughts make us take actions in our lives, and in turn, these actions shape our environments.

If my patient who is trying to stay sober from alcohol has a bad day at work, he goes home with an irritable mindset, gets in to an argument with his wife, comes out of his house for fresh air, and meets a friend who is going to a bar and asks him to accompany him. At this point, his id is trying to get an instant gratification of escape from the reality, which is not so happy. It would be very hard for him to say no to his friend according to his superego and because of the change of his brain chemistry due to alcohol abuse. If he chooses to go with his friend and get drunk, on the way home he might show even worse judgment under the influence of alcohol. He might drive, get in to an accident, and hurt himself or others. As you see in this process, all he is doing is choosing the wrong options one after another. As you can see, each and every decision we make in our lives creates an environment around us, and that environment becomes the foundation for the next reality and enables us to make the next decision. However, there is hope if we make some wrong turns. We can reverse this process with the help of our superior minds.

Freud also categorized the mind topographically. He named the mind, which is in the forefront working for our day-to-day experiences as the conscious mind, or readily accessible mind. The preconscious or subconscious mind is the second layer, which is accessible but not readily. The unconscious mind is the remote mind, and to access it, we have to achieve a state of trance. We can also look at this topographical categorization as based on the ability to access memory. The conscious mind may be able to remember things that happened in the recent past. The subconscious mind consists of the memories stored months ago. The unconscious mind deals with memories of the remote past.

We think we depend on the conscious mind for our day-to-day decisions and judgments. In actuality, the unconscious and subconscious play a huge part in it whether we accept it or not. We unconsciously react negatively at present when we have had a past negative encounter. We generalize and distort. When past trauma affects our cognition at present, we catastrophize. We follow the same parenting skills we learned from our parents, although we hated it while growing up. That's why we find two-third of parents who were physically or sexually abused in their childhood become abusers themselves, consciously or unconsciously.

Summary

1. Although we have modern knowledge about the brain and its functions, we are still unable to debunk the mystery of thinking processes.

2. That is the reason we have to resort to classify the mind (or thinking) according to Freudian structural and topographical theories of mind.

3. The id, ego, and superego most likely correlate with our lower brain and our higher brain, respectively.

4. Thoughts are originating from all different parts of the brain. Thoughts are being produced due to triggers from external environments and from our internal cues like hunger, anxiety, fear, etc.

5. It is extremely difficult to be mindful and discern thought patterns originating from the lower brain and higher brain. However, it's not impossible.

6. Our thinking process, or mind, defines us, and it's most likely a phenomenon originating from the chemical and electrical activities of the brain. However, in turn, it functions as the government of the body and brain, and the brain acts like a switchboard of the mind (or the thinking process).

CHAPTER 5

CARL G. JUNG: THE PSYCHIATRIST AND HIS CONCEPTS OF SYNCHRONICITY AND COLLECTIVE UNCONSCIOUS

Although C.G. Jung was a contemporary of Sigmund Freud who practiced and elaborated on Freud's psychoanalytic concepts, Jung has not been as popular a figure in academic psychiatry compared to Freud. His concepts were rather accepted by mass population in Western societies, especially in North America. Americanization of Jungian ideas is a slow-moving process. The key element separating Freud and Jung, for instance, was Jung's appeal to a growth-oriented dimension of the personality within the unconscious. Jung's theories were built on the idea that it is possible to experience a higher refined state of awareness than the normal waking condition.

While we are making such slow progress in the field the neuroscience, there is a proactive, demanding patient population looking for answers to their psycho-spiritual developments and the connection to well-being and developing ailments. The meeting interface of these two entities is that the consumer demands the delivery of the clinical services. It encompasses the entire spectrum of health professions, including medicine, nursing, psychology, and psychiatry. Jung's ideas are becoming more and more relevant and participating in the transformation of traditional science.

Carl Jung (1875–1961) was a lifelong resident of Switzerland. He developed an elaborate metapsychology that was every bit as detailed and formalized as Freud's. His construct of psychic apparatus differed than the Freudian structure of the id, ego, and superego. He integrated the structural and topographical concepts of mind and divided the unconscious in to a personal unconscious and a collective unconscious. He furthered to postulate that the personal unconscious is composed of complexes. These complexes are groups of unconscious ideas associated with particular emotionally toned events or experiences. Jung inferred this by his early word association studies where he found certain words in subjects evoked either intense or less reactions from his study subjects. He postulated complexes are built around genetically determined intrinsic psychic structures called archetypes.

Complexes can also be dependent on external events in one's life, depending on how much attention one wants to give to strengthen or weaken those complexes. He also noticed some complexes are more conscious than others, implying that the complexes can be part of both conscious and unconscious parts of the mind and that there is a fluidity when an unconscious complex is made aware by psychoanalyses and becomes a part of the conscious mind and vice versa.

Today we are aware that specific circuits of the brain only deal with specific memories. When we evaluate a patient, someone who underwent a traumatic event in early childhood or adulthood might have specific circuits of neuron trying to circumscribe that event so it does not affect the person's everyday functioning. However, whenever the person undergoes a triggering event similar to the past memory, the whole circuit can become reactivated, and the person's mental status destabilizes.

I want to give you an example of a patient of mine who was sent to me by his internist. The patient was a young man in his early thirties. He was married and trying to have children. He was recommended to have a psychiatric evaluation by his medical doctor, as he has been belligerent and verbally abusive to the children living in the same apartment complex. Sometimes while playing in the hallway the children would make too much noise, which he could not tolerate, so he would come out and yell and scream at the children. The children's parents complained to the superintendent of the apartment complex about his behavior, so it was recommended that he see a psychiatrist. Otherwise, he would have to move.

After a few sessions, the patient was able to recall an incident that had happened when he was ten years old. As a boy, he was living in an apartment complex with his parents. He used to play with the children on the first floor of that building. There was a treasure chest on that floor where they used to hide while playing hide-and-go-seek. The treasure chest could hold at least three or four children, and they could open and close it from inside. One day while playing, there were too many of them inside, and when the lid closed, they could not open it from inside. The children inside started screaming at the top of their lungs for at least half an hour until an adult rescued them. Although it took me a while to make my patient connect these two events, I instantly knew that every time he heard the noise of children screaming it activated his trauma of being in a treasure chest with three other children fighting for their lives. Although he was trying to have children, unconsciously he did not want children, as children cry and scream. The fear of re-activation of his anxiety symptoms, which he consciously and unconsciously tried to avoid, might have been the reason he was unable to have children.

Archetypes

Archetypes are the deeply embedded intrapsychic apparatus that are that foundation of complexes. There are as many archetypes as there are prototypic human situations. For example, every human being needs the nurturance of a mother figure because of his or her prolonged dependence on a primary caregiver. According to Jung, there is a mother archetype that develops into a complex, depending on the person's interactions and relationship with the mother or mother surrogate.

Jungian Unconscious

It has two layers: the personal unconscious, which coincides with Freudian unconscious, and the collective unconscious, which is the psychic DNA of the human race. Like physical DNA is composed of human physical characteristics and transmitted from generation to generation, collective unconscious serves as the mental DNA where the complexes can be built and personal unconscious can be created. Archetypes are situated in the collective unconscious. This theory coincides with Immanuel Kant's a priori theory.

Jungian Concept of Thinking

Jung categorized thinking into thinking in a conscious alert state of mind and thinking in a dream state. The dream state can be while we are asleep or while we are daydreaming. There were various hypotheses about thinking sprouting from many different philosophers, namely Anatole France, who emphasized that language is essential for our thinking process. However, Jodl denied the connection of language and thought because the same psychic fact can be expressed in different languages. From that, Jung drew that there is "an existence of super language thinking process." In *Psychology of Unconscious*, Jung hypothesized that the human race has a symbolic language; encoded in there is the "collective unconscious," and that encoded symbolic language, which is universal, is what we use when we are in a dream state. He states that "our thought consists for the great part of a series of images, one of which produces the other." It's a sort of passive dream state that higher animals are also capable of experiencing.

Synchronicity

Jung had a lifelong interest in the paranormal. This line of thinking had propelled him to describe the phenomenon of synchronicities. Synchronicity can be defined as meaningful coincidences that cannot be connected by a causal relationship. Some examples are as follows:

(1) A group of people singing in the church choir were to arrive at a certain time to practice in the church. Every one of them was late for some reason and escaped a fire that burnt down the church.

(2) Jung had a patient who had been in therapy with him without making any progress, as she was argumentative and resistant. One day she came in and stated that she had dreamt that a piece of golden, beetle-shaped jewelry was given to her. At the same moment while she was describing her dream, there was a sound at the window. Jung went to see what the sound was and found a golden scarab beetle trying to enter through the window. He caught it and brought it to his patient. He stated that it was the gift she had dreamt of. Since that time, the patient's resistance to therapy was dissipated, and she improved.

(3) In my life I have encountered numerous synchronicities. I could write another book describing them. However, I want to mention a few that are relevant to my practice and not personal. I was practicing as an outpatient psychiatrist in New York. The clinic was very busy and affiliated with a major city hospital. To obtain an

appointment, one had to schedule weeks or even months ahead. During one cold winter month with very short notice a blizzard started that lasted at least twenty-four hours. I made it to work somehow only to find out no patient had booked any appointments on that day. How was it possible that somehow months before people knew not to schedule an appointment on that day? A whole day without a patient in that clinic was unimaginable. That day we did not have any scheduled patients and no walk-ins due to the weather.

(4) I had a female patient who came with her husband to every visit. She told me a touching story. A few years earlier her husband had been very sick and in dire need of a liver transplant. He was facing death in few weeks if he did not get an immediate liver transplant. In few days, to their astonishment, they found out the surgeon who had been taking care of him had died in a car accident, and before he died, he requested his liver be given to his patient. To this date my patient's husband has been tolerating the transplant very well.

(5) I was involved in a car accident where I was not at fault. The person who hit me had two teenage girls and his wife in his car. No one was hurt, and we exchanged our insurance information. A few days later while I was at work, I had a teenager as my patient. When I was

doing a family session, I felt I had seen this family before. My patient's mother might have recognized me;
however, I did not recognize them at the time. It was
the family I had met few days earlier when my car was
hit. It makes me laugh at times. It was as if they were
in dire need of a psychiatrist, and that need had trans-
pired in to a collision in the form of an accident with a
psychiatrist.

(6) I just can't help giving this last one, which happened the morning I was writing this chapter. I was
at my favorite bakery waiting in line to get my coffee
and had been planning to finish this chapter that day.
I was deep in my thought when the attendant asked
me what I wanted. For some reason I told her I need
two cups of coffee, medium. A moment later I thought
to myself, *Why do I need two cups of coffee at the
same time?* I corrected myself and said I needed only
one. After the attendant gave me my coffee, I went to
the counter and put in my sugar and cream. I took a
sip, which tasted perfect. I left the bakery, and as I
was passing through the double door, something happened. I am not sure whether it was the wind or something else, but I dropped my coffee on the ground. I
rushed back and told the attendant that I had dropped
my coffee and asked for another one. She gave me
another one free of charge. I was so aggravated about

losing my perfect cup of coffee that I could not see the synchronicity until I started writing. How did I know that I actually needed two cups as I was going to lose one? Or was it that I created my reality by my own thinking process?

Synchronicities are very common phenomenon in everyone's life, which makes us wonder whether there is a higher conscious process at work always and if we able to connect with that process from time to time. We hear stories about people missing a flight and then that flight crash lands. So the question arises: Are some people able to avoid disasters and some are not because they are unable to tune in to the cues they are presented with? There is a series of questions we can ask based on these synchronicities we experience in our lives. These are as follows: Is it intuition or some special power that helps us avoid disasters at times? Is it our special relationship with God or a higher power that helps us? Is it an imbalanced mental status we are in that prohibits us from acknowledging the cue presented to us, so we walk into disasters? But someone who acknowledges that cue or is forced to make a drastic decision survives? Are we creating our own realities as we go with our right, wrong, or neutral mental status? Is it a phenomenon happening due to combination of all of the above?

Wolfgang Pauli, the Nobel Laureate on Synchronicity

Wolfgang Pauli was born in Vienna in 1900. He was a son of a medical doctor. He was an esteemed physicist who won a Nobel Prize in 1945 for his exclusion theory in quantum mechanics. He met Jung in a critical period of his life. They became friends and started to discuss synchronicity and published articles together in various journals on this topic. Pauli wanted to understand the marriage of matter and psyche and so did Jung. Together they ventured the world of dreams, quantum mechanics, and, of course, reality to come to a conclusion. However, their path was separated at one point, and synchronicity remained unexplained. Pauli tried to explain archetype and synchronicity in terms of quantum fields, their energy, and particles in them. He described that indestructible energy can be manifested as constant connection through effects and causality, and then it can be manifested as inconstant connection through contingence, equivalence, or meaning that is synchronicity. Pauli himself believed that synchronicity made it possible to begin a dialogue between physics and psychology in such a way that the subjective could be introduced into physics and objective in to psychology rather than looking exclusively at physics or psychology alone for solutions of nature's secrets.

While science deals in connections via forces and fields that are essentially causal in nature, Jungian synchronicity is acausal. The notion of an acausal connecting principle flies in the face of a compelling worldview that is based on a causally dominated universe where nothing takes place that does not have an ultimate cause.

Summary

1. Synchronicity is a very common phenomenon experienced by everyone from time to time in their lives. It connects events in a meaningful way but acausally. Carl Jung, the psychiatrist, and Wolfgang Pauli, the physicist, collaborated to understand and explain synchronicities. However, their efforts were unsuccessful to explain it in physical terms.

2. Does current progress and developments in quantum mechanics have the ability to explain synchronicity?

CHAPTER 6

THINKING PROCESS EXPLAINED WITH SOME CASE STUDIES

I have been a practicing psychiatrist for more than a decade. My profession is about understanding how people think and discern between an abnormal thinking pattern and a normal thinking pattern. I have treated and managed thousands of cases, as well as somehow participated in their lives as an advisor as events unfolded.

I mentioned earlier in chapter four how our brains function and probably give rise to the thinking process. This then becomes the ultimate government of our existence, and we are continuously being informed through our perceptual abilities and other factors in our lives and environment to make crucial decisions in our everyday lives.

In the past we have understanding about thoughts being produced automatically in the deeper parts of our brain. We have thoughts that are automatic, and we have no control of this process of constant popping up of images, visions, ideas, and memories like bubbles in a lake. Aaron Beck's concept of cognition and cognitive behavioral therapy revolutionized our understanding of the thinking processes. So we learned that thinking is partly automatic and partly a volitional process. That is, we are partly in control and partly not in control of our thoughts. Now if we look at the different parts of the brain roughly and hypothesize that the thinking process is the activity of all parts of the brain, then we can categorize the thinking as follows.

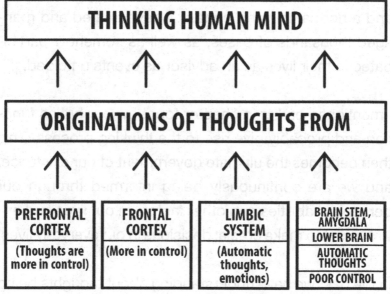

THINKING HUMAN MIND			
↑	↑	↑	↑
ORIGINATIONS OF THOUGHTS FROM			
↑	↑	↑	↑
PREFRONTAL CORTEX	**FRONTAL CORTEX**	**LIMBIC SYSTEM**	**BRAIN STEM, AMYGDALA**
			LOWER BRAIN
(Thoughts are more in control)	(More in control)	(Automatic thoughts, emotions)	AUTOMATIC THOUGHTS
			POOR CONTROL

Thoughts can originate from any part of the Brain. Higher the brain location, the more control we have on those throughts. The thoughts produced in the lower and deeper parts of brain are more automatic with poor or no control.

If we refer to the above picture, we see the lower part of the brain, which consists of our survival and emotional functions of our brain. So the thinking process, which will emanate from that part of the brain, will be mostly automatic—that is, not much is in our control. For example, when you are hungry, which is a basic survival instinct, you will encounter visual images of food in your thinking. It's like your car when needs the oil changed, the light starts to blink automatically. The same is true with the part of the brain that deals with emotion and stores emotional memories. When that's triggered, you are at the mercy of your automatic thinking process.

However, when your higher brain is producing thoughts and ideas, they are more in your control. So now if we give an example that you are hungry, your lower brain is constantly sending you signals of delicious unhealthy choices of food, while your higher mind will start producing thoughts of time, place, and the choices of food you should or should not have. However, you have to make choice regarding which is right or wrong for you. So if we consider that the lower brain produces thoughts that are primitive in nature and the higher brain produces the rational and reasonable thoughts, we can say that we are programmed to think in a right and a wrong way. Then our judgment and decision is a whole different area of importance. As we evolve mentally by educating and informing ourselves, the higher brain has more and more ammunition to give us clarity. Whether we listen to it and make a sound judgment or go by our reptilian instincts, that is what makes us different and unique. This process applies to every moment of our lives when we are making conscious decisions based on the right and wrong choices and taking actions on them.

I want to give few examples of some cases I took care of and how their thinking processes led them to certain circumstances in their lives and how they maneuvered through those circumstances by using their higher and lower brain. I have come across many people and was there with them as events unfolded in their lives. Here I will talk about two women who somehow faced similar circumstances in their lives, but due to their different decision-making processes, their lives were directed in two completely different directions. One was successful in materialistic terms, while the other was not so successful. I want to clarify I am not here to judge anyone. I would just like to state the facts.

For confidentiality purposes, I will not mention any names, so I will refer them as Ms. A and Ms. B. Both of them had multiple similarities. They were both Asian immigrants of similar age. They were both married, and both of them had to move from New York to relocate in the same state temporarily before moving back to New York.

First I will tell Ms. A's story. Ms. A was a thirty-year-old Asian immigrant. She was married with two children, a nine-year-old boy and a six-year-old girl. Her husband was ten years older than her and had some medical issues. Due to their recent immigration, they were having a lot of conflict in their relationship. Her husband having some medical issues and was unable to find appropriate work. She started working but had not been happy with her job, so she was constantly looking for something new. Through a friend, she got a job offer in a different state. She and her family became excited and left New York somewhat impulsively only to find the other state did not have subway system, and neither of them knew how to drive.

Ms. A began her new job and found her boss to be very helpful. She started using public transportation to go to work and to come back home. A few months later her boss started offering her rides to and from her home. Initially, she rejected the rides, but Ms. A's husband suffered from heart issues and became hospitalized at that time, so she started accepting rides from her boss. Her boss started asking for sexual favors. She became enamored and succumbed to an extramarital affair. Her husband recovered from his ailments and found out about the affair. He decided to move back to New York, and Ms. A agreed, so they

moved back. However, Ms. A started having symptoms of depression, as she started feeling guilty and
ashamed about her affair. At that point, she came to
see me. The course of her illness fluctuated, and she
remained in treatment for few years and required hos-
pitalization at one point.

Now I will tell Ms. B's story. Ms. B was a thirty-two-
year-old Asian immigrant. She was married with a
ten-year-old boy and a six-year-old girl. She and her
husband were working in New York. All of a sudden
her husband had a better job opportunity in a faraway
state. Ms. B became very concern about her being
a single parent in the absence of her husband. She
started looking for a job in the same state where her
husband had found work. Unfortunately, she was only
able to find work in a neighboring state. She decided
to move there, while her husband worked in the neighboring state. While she was adjusting in a new job
environment, she became friends with her colleagues
and her supervisors. Her relationship with her husband
became very strained because of their separation. She
was tempted to form extramarital and emotional relationships; however, she decided against it. Instead,
she quit her job and moved back to New York. After a
brief separation, her husband also moved back to New
York to join her.

If we analyze both of these cases, we see a lot of similarities in terms of their life circumstances. They were both vulnerable and were almost pushed to circumstances beyond their control. However, Ms. A showed poor judgment when she went by her lower brain influence, while Ms. B showed much better judgment by leaving the job environment that was not serving her and her children's interests. Ms. A developed depression due to the shame and guilt she suffered, while Ms. B's mental reaction to her circumstances resolved without any complications in few weeks.

In these two examples, the suddenness of the change in their lives also gave rise to questions regarding why people have to deal with similar circumstances in their lives. Are they being tested by those circumstances and how they make their decisions and enjoy or suffer the consequences?

I want to give another example of two other patients whose date of birth was exactly the same. However, they had different ethnicities and religions. I will name them Ms. C and Ms. D. They both came to me right after they lost their younger sisters. Both of the patients' younger sisters were suffering from chronic physical illnesses, and both of the patients were involved in their care. When Ms. C's sister passed away, she started experiencing a major depressive disorder. She was unable to work. She started taking medications with some improvements in her mental symptoms, but her physical health started to deteriorate. She developed a heart condition and had to go through open-heart surgery in a matter of six months after she lost her sister. However, Ms. D received bereavement counseling and did very well. She did not require any medications. She improved after five to six sessions of psychotherapy. The difference between these two patients was their religiosity and practicing of their religions. Ms. C did not practice her religion actively, whereas Ms. D had strong faith and was actively practicing her religion.

If we further analyze the first two cases, we see that both Ms. A and Ms. B had to move to the other states and had both been unhappy in their marriages. We can assume most of the time they were preoccupied with the thinking originating from the lower brain, which deals with the emotional processes related with their survival. They needed the emotional support from their partners, and when it was absent, they were presented with options to deviate and form other relationships or be self-sufficient and dependent on their own resources. Under the circumstances, they were both put into situations where the core values of their beings were tested. In case of Ms. B, however, she was ultimately able to be influenced by the thinking processes of her higher mind and did not take the easy way out. In case of Ms. C, she was emotionally driven, leading her to be severely depressed after losing her sister, and ultimately, her poor mental functioning gave way to further physical ailments. In contrast, Ms. D used her higher brain functions, namely resilience, religiosity, and spirituality, to cope with her loss, which eventually restored her physical and mental well-being.

Summary

The following questions arise after this discussion:

1. Do we create our own life circumstances by our specific thinking processes?

2. Can we infer that similar kinds of thinking patterns give rise to similar kinds of life situations, as we saw in the examples of Ms. A and Ms. B, as well as Ms. C and Ms. D?

CHAPTER 7

MODERN TECHNOLOGY

For my own understanding I wanted to recap and write a chapter on modern technological advances. While we are grappling to be knowledgeable about mental processes, there is a parallel revolution happening in the field of artificial intelligence (AI). We are building robots, drones, and satellites and sending probes to other planets. Are we on the verge of taken over by AI?

It started with Guglielmo Marconi and his invention of the radio. Marconi utilized electromagnetic radiation, also called ether or radio waves, and began working on his idea of wireless telegraphy. This was not a new idea. At the time, numerous scientists were already working on radio waves, namely Heinrich Hertz who demonstrated one could produce and detect electromagnetic radiation now known as the radio wave, or aetheric waves or hertzian waves. However, Marconi developed portable transmitters, or receivers, of radio waves, and rest is history in the world of communications.

Next we created television, which functions in similar ways. There is the transmission tower sending electromagnetic radiations, or waves, in certain frequencies, which can be captured by these receivers called television or radio. Then came the era of the Internet. Our interaction became global. We are now communicating with each other at the speed of light. We are storing a wealth of information in one small microchip of a computer. We are able to work in an interactive grid and communicate with each other provided we are connected with a source computer or a satellite.

If we try to make a comparison between the human intelligence versus artificial intelligence, we will see many similarities and dissimilarities as well.

Human Mind/Intelligence	Artificial Intelligence
Similarities	
Energy comes from food	Energy source is electricity from lithium batteries or a source, which is converted to an electrical phenomenon
Making decisions, performing actions; storing memories, remembering	Only functioning according to programming, storing information
Human mind can be influenced by other minds, dogma, and culture.	Constantly under control of humans

Brain appears to be the switch board of human mind.	There is a switchboard connecting different parts and functioning as a whole; chips, microchips working as a whole
Dissimilarities	
All information received becomes an experience and perception and is then stored	Information is not experienced; the machine has no perception
Able to feel emotions and understand abstract concepts	Unable to feel emotions or understand abstract concepts
Has creativity, vision, and willpower	Has none of this; controlled by human
The human mind is alive	Machine; nonliving

The above comparison table differentiates between human intelligence and artificial intelligence. As we see, the computers are not alive. They cannot experience or perceive any information. They are just storage equipment and function according to the way they were originally programmed by humans.

This era of biological research has created genetically modified organisms, or GMOs; the cloning of animals; and stem cell research promising revolutionary techniques to heal ailments. Does it all indicate that we are being able to create life on this earth? It seems like we are playing God at times. This is especially true in the health care field through the adopting of biomechanics and nanotechnologies, which are able to prolong lives.

We are cutting and pasting genomic codes and trying to improve the size of crops. We are cloning one cell from another and allowing it to grow in to an animal. We are fertilizing human ovum in a test tube and allowing the product to grow in a surrogate mother. All we are doing is mixing and matching, splicing and splitting in the genomic level and coming up with what many perceive as better products. However, so far we have not been able to assemble one cell from scratch with its nucleus, plasma, mitochondria, DNA, or RNA as a functioning, living organism.

Quantum Mechanics

Quantum mechanics deals with the subatomic structures and energy fields. When we are discussing the mind, we are also talking about the constant electrical firing of 100 billion neurons. I have been fascinated by ongoing research in physics and have been trying to keep up, although I am not a physicist. Recent experiments in particle physics and the creating of the Higgs boson proved the theory by Nobel Prize-winning physicist Peter Higgs about an ever-present field of energy that permeates the entire universe and endows massless particles with mass. It's revolutionary.

A basic outline on quantum mechanics according to my understanding is as follows:

As we know, the atom is the building block of matter. An atom is composed of subatomic particles, like electrons, protons, and neutrons. Electrons have the least mass. Protons and neutrons are made of quarks and are heavier than electrons. The heavier ones are the particles with mass and are vulnerable for decay, and the lighter they are, the longer they exist, some forever. A century-long experiment on electrons did not reveal any decay in their structure. Electrons are known as elementary particles, having a mass which is $1/1,836^{th}$ that of a proton. It also has a spin. Electrons can transform into wave and particle form. When in particle form, they can collide with other particles, and when in wave form, they can be diffracted like light. Physical phenomenon involving electrons play an essential role in our lives, such as electricity, magnetism, and thermal conductivity. An electron generates a magnetic field while moving. Electrons radiate and absorb energy in the form of photons when accelerated. Electrons are involved in many applications, such as electronics, welding, cathode-ray tubes, electron microscopes, radiation therapy, lasers, gaseous ionization detectors, and particle accelerators.

I am intentionally leaving out the larger particles like proton, neutron, etc. My focus in this subject is only on the elementary particles that resonate with the mental or biological processes I described in the previous chapters. I am talking about the electrical phenomenon that goes on in animal minds, which is mostly mediated through electron and electricity—at least that's what current research implies.

It started around in 1900 with Max Planck with his quantum hypothesis. He observed the black body radiation along with other physicists like Michael Faraday and Gustav Kirchhoff. Plank came up with the hypothesis that energy is radiated and absorbed in distinct quanta that precisely matched the observed patterns of black body radiation. Later Albert Einstein proposed a quantum-based theory to explain the photoelectric effect.

According to Planck, $E=h\nu$, where h is Planck constant. Energy is proportional to its frequency (ν).

In 1905 Albert Einstein interpreted Plank's quantum theory realistically and used it to explain photoelectric effect. He won the Nobel Prize in 1921 for his work. Einstein further developed this idea that an electromagnetic wave such as light could also be described as a particle (later called a photon) with a discrete quantum of energy that is dependent on its frequency.

From Einstein's simple postulation was born a flurry of debating, theorizing, and testing; thus, the entire field of quantum physics emerged. It was found that subatomic particles and electromagnetic waves are neither simply particles nor waves but have certain properties of each. This originated the wave-particle duality concept.

If we generalize our knowledge so far, we come up with the following sequence of events on an atomic level: **mass to atom to electron to movement of electron to electromagnetic field to light to photon (it can exist as a particle or as waves of light.)**

If we reverse the above sequence of events, we get: **photon (light wave/particle) to electron (particle with slight mass) to atom mass.**

The next chapter of quantum physics has been dealing with the problem of how this quanta of energy, or massless particles (photons), gain their masses. It was observed that some elementary particles, such as photons, are massless, but electrons have a mass. So there has to be a field that supplies the mass to these massless particles. Peter Higgs came up with the idea of the Higgs field and hypothesized about a particle that is elementary in nature but has mass and no spin.

Higgs is a Nobel Laureate of 2013 for his work on proposing the existence of a new particle, which is called Higgs Boson, detection of which became the greatest goal of quantum physicists. To attain that goal, billions of dollars were spent to make eighteen-mile-long hadron colliders where protons were allowed to collide with each other. Super sensitive computers were built to detect the newly formed particles.

Not going into details, I want to mention what boson is. Elementary particles are divided into two broad groups: fermions and bosons. Boson was the name given to certain particles to commemorate the work of Satyendra Nath Bose, a Bengali physicist from Undivided India, who mainly identified these subatomic particles so that Einstein and other physicist could work on his concepts.

Fermions are the particles that have less than one integral spin—that is, one-half or two-thirds and so on—and obey the Pauli exclusion principle. But boson has either zero, one, or two spin and does not follow the exclusion principle. Both of these broad spectrums of particles can be with mass or be massless. Like a photon, which is a boson, has a spin of one but is massless. While an electron is a fermion with one-half integral spin and has a slight mass. On the contrary, Higgs boson was hypothesized to be a boson with a mass. It was also hypothesized that the massless particle (i.e., photon) will gain the mass from Higgs field. Higgs field is a field of energy that permeates the entire universe and provides mass to these massless particles, namely photons/quanta of energy. This hypothesis also clarifies the big bang theory. It was a puzzle how the big bang, or the explosion of energy, happened that led to the formation of mass in the universe. So physicists have been trying to prove this hypothesis and were successful in identifying Higgs boson and the presence of Higgs field, (which is analogous to ether) on July 4, 2012.

Inadvertently, Higgs boson has been named the God particle. One of the physicists became frustrated and initially called it the goddamn particle but later chose to call it the God particle.

Summary

1. Most technological advances are based on the elec-tromagnetic force field and radiation. The transmission and reception through devices like radio, television, and wireless telephones use the same force.

2. Artificial intelligence, although making headline news, is still under the domain of human control.

3. Quantum mechanics made revolutionary progress by identifying the Higgs field in reality and creating Higgs boson, an elementary particle with mass from photon a massless particle.

4. Proof of existence of Higgs field, which is a field with everlasting energy also called plasma that permeates the entire universe and provides the necessary mass to the massless particles, is leading us to acknowledge an omnipotent source of power and energy that never decays an never dies. Did we really find God in the God particle?

CHAPTER 8

PSYCHIATRY AND MEDICAL SCIENCE

In 1946, the World Health Organization defined health as follows: "Health is a state of complete physical, mental and social well-being and not merely the absence of disease or infirmity."

The above definition of *health* sheds light on certain perspectives on the concept of health. If we elaborate on this, we see it implies that health is the ultimate physical and mental state that we have to achieve and put in effort to sustain. It also implies there is a spectrum of physical and mental conditions that might be prevalent before someone actually develops a disease condition. If we are able to identify those states and some traits that make us resilient, we might be able to prevent major diseases and improve the quality of our lives. Because of this paradigm shift in the concept of health, preventive health is getting attention all over the world. Not only the infectious diseases, but cancer, heart disease, type 2 diabetes, high cholesterol, and emotional disturbances, including, depression, anxiety, and even schizophrenia are being attributed to environmental factors and stress-related changes in gene expression. The bottom line is that modern medicine is identifying the core level problems as people's lifestyles and how these different lifestyles affect the well-being of people versus the slow progression to a disease state. I am not including the disease conditions that are present from birth or acquired due to pure genetic anomaly. I am talking about the majority of diseases that are deemed preventable by changing one's lifestyle or that the progression or recurrence can even be stopped by appropriate mental and physical intervention.

Now a little bit about the mind-body conundrum phenomenon: Is the mind equally responsible for a mental disease as a medical condition? The interface of psychiatry and medical science is gaining tremendous importance in twenty-first-century medical science. Stress reaction to immunity and hormonal imbalance have been attributed to temporary or permanent changes in to one's DNA leading to abnormal protein formation resulting in multiple disease processes. In an attempt to understand the potential mechanisms of the effect of stress on illnesses involving the immune system, researchers had focused considerable attention on the effects of stress on a variety of immune parameters in laboratory animals and humans. Prospective studies on upper respiratory tract infections verified by a physician's diagnosis or by biological methods of evidence indicate that stressful life events can increase the susceptibility to infectious diseases in humans.

Mind and body concept of disease production has been present since ancient times. In 10,000 BC the primitive society believed disease was caused by evil powers, and in order to achieve wellness, one had to use spiritual exercise like exorcism. In 400 BC Socrates defined health as a whole. He stated, "As it is not proper to cure the eyes without the head, nor the head without the body, so neither it is proper to cure the body without the soul." Hippocrates stated, "In order to cure human body, it is necessary to have the knowledge of whole of things."

In the Middle Ages (500 to 1450 BC) mysticism and religion dominated medicine. Sinning was the cause of mental and physical illness. From 1800 to 1900 modern laboratory-based medicine emerged, as we were able to see microorganisms, and psychic influences in the body were completely rejected. From 1900 until the present, Freud's psychoanalytic theory conceptualized psychosomatic medicine, which explains the psychic influences in physical symptoms and producing psychiatric conditions such as conversion disorder and somatization disorder. In 1927 Walter Cannon demonstrated the physiological concomitants of some emotions and the important role of autonomic nervous system in producing those somatic physiological responses. In 1958 Adolf Meyer formulated the biopsychosocial approach to patients. In 1977 George Engel coined the term *Biopsychosocial*, which then became the model to assess, diagnose, and formulate a treatment plan for a psychiatric patient in a psychiatric practice.

If we just look at cardiovascular disease—that is, heart disease—numerous data is available today that indicates psychological factors play a significant role on sudden cardiac death, cardiac ischemia, and arrhythmias. In 1964 the term *psychoneuroimmunology* was coined to identify the field of investigation directed at understanding how behavior and mental status affect immune function. It was found that behavioral states such as disturbed sleep function, examination stress, loneliness, unemployment, marital discord, divorce, bereaved spouses, and many more can cause immune suppression, leading to variety of disease conditions, including gastrointestinal issues, autoimmune diseases, psychiatric illnesses, and even cancer.

It is pertinent to say that twenty-first-century medicine has been transformed to acknowledge and incorporate mental processes to identify the causality and treatment of physical ailments. In the meantime, a growing body of research is pointing toward certain psychological traits, including optimism, wisdom, creativity, religiosity, and spirituality, are associated with better medical and psychiatric health outcome.

I would like to give a brief overview about these mental strengths. Optimism is one's positive way of looking into the future and expecting favorable outcome. Wisdom is a virtue that is multifaceted, incorporating one's experiences in life and applying all the knowledge gained. There are subcomponents of wisdom, which are prosocial attitude, compassion, empathy, and altruism. Creativity in the form of music, art, dance, expressive writing, visual arts, photography, etc. can boost well-being. In the past two decades it has been noticed that religiosity and spirituality have been polarized. However, the common factor for both of them is focusing on a sacred entity (God, transcendence, the ultimate reality). Religion is a more structured and institutionalized form of spirituality. Spirituality is more individualized, but nonetheless, it is a transcendent relationship with an entity beyond physical, psychological, or social dimensions of life. In a recent survey, 96 percent of adults reported that they believe in God and that religion is the most important influence in their personal lives. A growing body of evidence-based medicine links spirituality and religiosity with better outcomes in disease conditions and for general well-being.

Anatomically speaking, if we try to correlate this mental phenomenon such as optimism, wisdom, creativity, resilience, spirituality, and religiosity, we find our superior brain is responsible for these functions, namely different parts of prefrontal and frontal cortex, temporal lobe, and parietal cortex. To some extent, the limbic system and amygdala are involved as well.

It is evident that modern medicine has come a long way to prove Socrates's presumption that we need to incorporate both body and mind together to understand a disease process fully, and if we want to cure it successfully, we have to pay attention to both. Not only the disease processes, but modern medicine concludes that well-being or the state of health is an optimum condition where mind and body chemistry is rightfully balanced so that we can fight off occurrences of disease and in case in the middle of a disease process stops its progression or recurrence.

Summary

1. The common concept of health has changed from time to time. We have evolved into a twenty-first-century technology-infused health care system, but we are going back to Socrates's original hypothesis of mind-body integration. A larger and larger body of evidence points toward that fact.

2. Positive mental attributes mentioned above play a significant role in the healing process of both mental and physical conditions.

3. The positive psychological traits that play an important role in the healing process are mostly in the domain of our superior brain.

4. Can we infer from these findings that if we nurture and practice superior brain qualities such as optimism, wisdom, resilience, creativity, religiosity, and spirituality in our lives that we will be able to achieve a better state of health and prevent disease?

5. And why not, depending on our superior brain qualities in other aspects of our lives as well, which might allow us to live a quality life and might allow us to make this world a better place for another.

CHAPTER 9

SPIRITUAL MECHANICS

When I started writing this book, I had a vague notion where I was going. I had glimpses of what was coming next, but I could not see the big picture. Now that I am trying to assimilate what I learned, I feel amazed. I wanted to find common grounds for philosophy, religion, and modern science in describing mental phenomenon. It appears that all these three dimensions of knowledge point toward similar facts about mind. Modern science describes the thinking process analogous to 1 trillion neurons of electrical activity mediated by electrons moving to and fro. Electrons are almost massless and eternal. All religions say the soul is immortal. The same concept was echoed by the philosophers for centuries.

Let's start with the realm of philosophy. Discussion about these wise men of old revealed that most of them were spiritual except for skeptics like David Hume and his followers. Most of these philosophers believed in a superior mind, and some of them, especially the Milesians, saw spirits everywhere, including plants, in the animal kingdom, and even in inanimate objects. They believed the spirit of God is everywhere.

The chronological advancement in philosophy naturally progressed to "know thyself" from the era of Socrates until Descartes who defined the mind and postulated a theory of dualism. Dualism has been misinterpreted and misconstrued due to lack of knowledge in that era about mind and actual mental processes. "Although psychosomatic scholars have incriminated René Descartes for creating mind body dualism that prevented the development of integrated models of psychosomatic relations in the evolution of modern medicine, that conclusion may be a misunderstanding of Cartesian theory. Careful analysis of Descartes ideas reveals that he did not rigidly split the mind from body, but regarded mental forces as interacting with physical. Brown proposed that rather than denying theoretical mind body interactions, Descartes actually facilitated them." (Kaplan and Sadock, volume two)

CONCEPT OF MIND
Structure of Mind according to Descartes's Dualism, Modern science and World's Major religions.

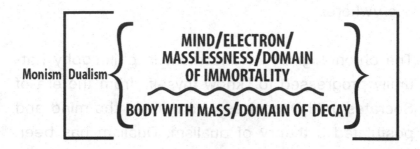

Modern concepts of mind, which I discussed in chapter four, lead us to believe the mind is nothing but 1 trillion neurons' constant electrical firing. Electrical firing is analogous to electrons in the subatomic level as a form of energy moving to and fro. So what is happening in a living organism is that the biological processes transfer energy to the part of the body called the nervous system/ brain, which is full of insulated, live electric wires leading to a constant flow of electrons leading to this phenomenon called the mind, which is ultimately serving as the government of the organism. So we see René Descartes concept of dualism was not farfetched at all. If we analyze our knowledge on the basis of quantum mechanics, we see the energy in the form of food coming down to the minutest level and converting in to almost a massless state that is the electron. This massless state also leads to an unperishable state of matter. Electrons have a slight mass, but after a decade-long observation, we did not find any decay in electrons.

Based on the above discussion, mind and body depend on each other, but as if they are in two different dimensions or planes. The body is in the materialistic realm of mass, and the mind is in the realm of no mass. If we go back to the realm of religion and try to recall about the concept of the soul, most religions say the soul/mind is unperishable, immortal. Moreover, Koranic literature distinctively divides mind and body into two different domains. The body resides in the plane of Khalq, or the plane of mass and matter, and the mind or soul is at Amar, the plane of spirits (or no mass).

If we recall from chapter eight, the sequence of events giving rise to mass in this universe is as follows: **light (photons in wave or particle form) to Higgs field to Higgs boson (particle with mass) to atom to mass.**

In the realm of religion, we have discussed how God has proclaimed that all his creation is made of his *nur*—that is, his light. Now if we go back to quantum mechanics, we see that subatomic particle photons, which are also light particles, are capable of changing in to wave forms and particle forms. From chapter seven, we can go over the definition of Higgs field again. Presence of this field has been hypothesized by Peter Higgs, a Nobel Laureate. It took thirty years of experimentation to prove the existence of this field. This is a field of everlasting energy permeating the entire universe. The massless particle photon can gain mass going through this field. Presence of this field also proves the big bang theory of creation of the universe. Scientist has wondered if the big bang happened, but who or what supplied the enormous energy for that bang? Now they can put two and two together and explain the big bang phenomenon of creation.

Now if we look at the qualities of God mentioned in different religious books, especially in the Koran, we see God describes himself in the following ways: "As Samad or ever-present or eternal," "An Nur the light," and "Al Basit, The expander of the Universe." These are a few qualities that are meeting the criteria of this energy field permeating the entire universe, which is the eternal source of energy that also made of particles of light. Moreover, he is also recognizing himself as the expander of the universe, and we already know that the universe is expanding. This makes us wonder: have we actually found God in Higgs field? We only need to assign a mind to this energy field. Then we might call it our creator who created everything from his light/*nur*. Let's discuss how we can do this. As we know, we are the living proof of a being who is living and experiencing the world around us tangibly with the help of our minds, however unable to fathom the mind itself. We had concluded that the immediate step before the mind phenomenon is the force field created by the constant firing of electrons in our brain. At the same token, we can hypothesize this ever-present, omnipotent energy field should possess a mind like we do, which is the superior mind or the mind of God.

Similarities of Mind of God and Human Mind

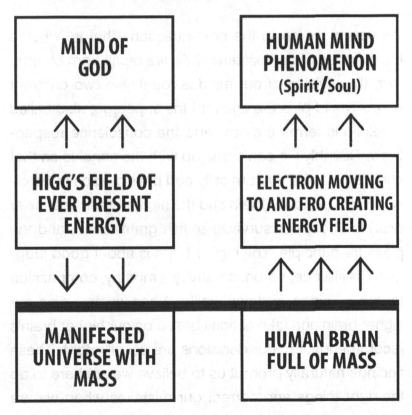

If we recall from the previous chapters, the philosophers, the prophets, the saints, and the basis of most of the religions is the faith in this omnipotent energy source. He is called Brahma in Hinduism, Allah in Islam, and God in Christianity. He might have different names, but his qualities are the same. I believe if we assimilate all the information from religions, philosophy, and modern science, we might be able to prove the existence of a superior mind from whom we are drawing all this knowledge time and time again. All the wisdom is leading us back to him.

We can move on to the next question—that is, what is the purpose of our existence? As we recall from chapter four, the division of our mind is roughly in two different parts. The id plus the ego and the superego, also called in religious terms the *nafs* and the conscience respectively. Roughly we can come up with the conclusion that our brain can be anatomically and physiologically, be divided into the lower brain and the higher brain. The lower brain is about our survival, selfish gratification, and the pleasure principle. The higher brain is about good judgment, resilience, vision, creativity, empathy, compassion for other beings, and spirituality. When we are using our higher brain and take actions based on our higher brain's recommendation, our decisions are usually right. These findings naturally prompt us to believe we are here to do the right things and correct our mistakes when we are wrong. These right and wrong might not be generalized but are unique for that specific individual. That's why we see that most religions prohibit the judging of one another.

It appears that we do have a purpose! Otherwise, why would our minds be biologically programmed in to a lower and a higher mind?

When we are making decisions and acting on it based on our fear (amygdala/lower brain), greed/selfish gratification (lower brain), emotions (hippocampus/lower brain), or self-survival (lower brain), ignoring the need of other beings, individually or collectively, the end result is not so good. However, when we use our knowledge/logic (frontal cortex/higher brain), empathy (cingulate cortex/higher brain), or compassion (cingulate cortex/higher brain), we tend to make decisions that fare well for everyone involved, individually and collectively.

These wrongs and rights might or might not correlate with our societal wrongs and rights. These wrongs and rights are unique for each and every one of us according to our own mental makeup. How do we go about and discern our own right from wrong and identify the right action or decision on a moment by moment basis in the drama of our lives?

I believe that is the test my mother was talking about when I was young. There are numerous life experiences and situations we face from the time we are born. According to Nobel Laureate and economist Lloyd Shapley's game theory, our lives' events are dependent on other people's right and wrong decisions. Amid all these influences, how do we stand our ground dealing with our own emotions, identify and fight our tendency to take the easy way out, and identify and fight our tendency to harm other beings for our own material gain in an overt or covert way? How do we identify these tendencies and constantly fight vigilantly to do the right thing?

That is a theme that needs elaborate discussions and might be a theme for a future book.

BIBLIOGRAPHY

1. The Holy Quran, By M.A Haleem Eliasii, translated by Mohammed Marmuaduke Pickthall.

2. *The Bible, Qur'an and Science*, by Dr. Maurice Bucaille.

3. *Psychiatry and Religion, The Convergence of Mind and Spirit* edited by, James k. Boehnlein, MD, MSc.

4. *Positive Psychiatry*, a clinical handbook, edited by Dillip V Jeste MD, Barton W. Palmer, PhD.

5. *Brain and Culture, Neurobiology, Ideology and Social Change*, Bruce E. Wexler.

6. *Psychology of Unconscious*, C.G. Jung

7. *Synchronicity the Marriage of Matter and Psyche* by F. David Peat.

8. *Jung on Synchronicity and the Paranormal*, by Rodrick Main.

9. *Greek Philosophy, Thales to Aristotle.* Edited by Reginald E. Allen.

10. René Descartes, Meditations and other metaphysical writings.

11. Kaplan & Sadock's comprehensive textbook of Psychiatry volume I and II.